RUDE AWAKENING
A WARRIOR SUB-CULTURE

PETRAVICIUS

Rude Awakening: A Warrior Sub-Culture

Copyright 2025 by Erik Petravicius

All rights reserved, this book or any portion thereof may not be reproduced or used in any manner whatsoever without the express written permission of the publisher except for the use of brief quotations in a book review.

ISBN: 978-1-966111-12-2

Publisher E & M Renegade Creative works, LLC

Dedication

"Dedicated to my son Darius, who has endured countless lofe lectures from me with patience and heart."

Table of Contents

The Toe Chronicles 1
The Kind of Women I Like 5
The World & My Bad Boy 9
I Am Seven 13
The Board 17
The Queen 21
The King's Burden 25
He Changed 29
Boots 33
Controlled Chaos 37
Returning Fire 41
Capacity 45
Good Man 49
The Moth 51
Rest In Peace for Today I Die 53
Cold Burn 55
She Hung There 61
Loving the Broken 65
Look Away 69
After the Fall 73
Unashamed 77
What Hurt Made 81
The Third Island 85

Like No One Else 89

The Discipline of Peace 91

Build Yourself 95

The Higher Ground 99

The Warrior Who Knows Himself 103

Character Is the Spine 107

On Loving Through the Flaws 109

Higher Ground is a Choice 111

The Ground Rules 113

A Man Dies When His Purpose Does 115

Inheritance Is Character First, Results Second 117

Quiet Builders 119

The Duty of a Man Who Thinks Beyond Himself 121

The God of Men Who've Seen Violence 123

Redemption Is a Discipline 127

Accountability Is a Form of Prayer 129

The Climb Back 131

Rules for Rising 133

The Toe Chronicles

Pain changes as you age.
When you're young, pain feels like a challenge.
By thirty-five, it feels personal.
By forty… it feels like your body is plotting a coup.

It starts small.
Neck stiff.
Back sore.
Knees sound like popcorn.
Ankles negotiate every step like hostage demands.
Hands, wrists, elbows — the whole assembly line starts unionizing.

Then one morning, pain looks around and says:

"Where else can we fuck with him?"

And in the back of your nervous system,
one little cell raises its hand like an overachiever in school:

"The toe.
Hit him in the toe."

Toe pain is spiritual pain.
Stub your toe and watch your soul leave your body
like it's clocking out early.

There is no anger like the anger of toe pain.
Not heartbreak.
Not betrayal.
Not war.
Toe pain sends a man straight into the void.

And I swear there's a demon waiting in every doorway,
sitting there like:

*"He thinks he's safe.
Watch this."*

I don't care how tough a man is.
You could be a Navy SEAL, Marine Recon,
fought wars, jumped out of planes,
deadlifted your demons—

Stub your toe, and you instantly become
a barefoot toddler with trust issues.

Pain evolves.
Bodies betray.
But one thing remains universal:

The toe always wins.

The Kind of Women I Like

People always ask me
what kind of women I like.

Truth is —
I like women.
Period.

I've seen beauty in every style God ever printed:

Slim, thick, gym-curved,
soft, plush, BBW queen energy,
tall like a runway,
short like trouble,
all of it.

Bodies are like fingerprints —
and I respect the art form of creation.

Some men pretend they don't look —
I don't pretend.
I admire.

Blue eyes that look like ocean water after war,
Brown eyes that feel like home,
Green eyes that know secrets,
Hazel eyes that say *"I'm sweet until I'm not."*

Even the wild ones —
cross-eyed, crazy-eyed,
the ones who've cried just enough to get dangerous —
men underestimate crazy at their own risk.
Crazy women love hard and fight harder.
Testosterone learns humility.

And yeah, I'm an ass man.
God built the glute for survival
— and worship.

That's science.

But listen…

There are **three deal-breakers** in this life:

1. Bad teeth
Because if your mouth looks like a battlefield
your words probably are too.

2. Bad attitude
If I wanted to wake up to someone yelling every day,
I'd go back to the Army.
At least the Army feeds you and teaches discipline.

Some women just want to recruit you
into their emotional combat unit.
Nah. I already served.

3. Bad energy down below
and no, I'm not explaining that
because grown men already know the truth about wounds and wellness down there.

A man can be loyal, gentle, spiritual —
but he's still a **man**.
Biology doesn't care about social theory.

Listen —
Women are powerful.
I admire them.
I love them.
I laugh with them.
I war with life beside them.

But not every woman deserves access.
And not every man should be begging for it.

I'm not chasing validation.
I am the validation.

I don't need every queen —
I just match with the right ones.
Clean teeth, calm spirit, real feminine energy,
and a body that tells the truth it lives in.

That's the criteria.
Not complicated.
Just standards.

A king doesn't lower his crown.
He waits for the woman who knows how to wear hers.

The World & My Bad Boy

Some days, if we're being honest,
people just suck.

Not everyone —
but enough to make you wonder
if God ever took customer feedback.

Most folks walk around powered by ego,
insecurity,
and whatever algorithm told them who to be that morning.

Everybody wants to be a victim,
nobody wants to be accountable.
They want attention,
not growth.
Comfort, not truth.

And yeah, for a minute,
the world almost had me fooled.
Made me think I should soften up,
behave,
play nice,
tuck away the part of me built for storms.

But I remembered something:

The world doesn't reward softness.
It respects strength, clarity, and self-possession.

So I called my grit back.
I called that inner wolf home.
Not the reckless version —
the disciplined one.
The version who's lived, fought, bled, loved, and learned.
The one who can shake the room by walking into it quietly.

People talk about "bad boys."

That's not it.
I'm not interested in chaos.
I'm interested in **presence**.
Self-respect.
Boundaries.
Standards.

I'm not here to be liked.
I'm here to be **real**.

And if that makes some people uncomfortable,
that's fine.
Comfort never built a king.
Comfort never built a warrior.
Comfort never built a soul worth remembering.

The world can keep its noise.
I'll keep my edge —
and my peace.

Some will fear it.
Some will misunderstand it.
The right ones will respect it.

That's the beauty of truth:

You don't need everyone.
You just need your people.

And the rest?

Yeah…
they can keep sucking.

I Am Seven

I am Seven.

Not by ego
not by fantasy
not by need for worship—
but by the weight I carry
and the discipline that forged me.

Completion is not comfort.
Completion is burden.
Responsibility.
Awareness you cannot return from.

I am not here to be adored.
I am here to **lead**—
first myself,
then the world I am entrusted with.

King is not a title.
King is a state achieved
when a man conquers the only real enemy:
his own weakness.

Women do not follow kings
because they are commanded.
They follow kings
because kings do not fracture under pressure,
do not bargain with doubt,
do not fold when the world turns hostile.

Purpose before pleasure.
Duty before desire.
Legacy before ego.

My Queens—
the ones who hear this
and feel no fear in surrendering

not their strength,
but their *chaos*—
they are not beneath me.
They walk beside me.
They choose alignment
because they know a throne is not given,
it is answered.

The world does not need softness.
It needs men who are dangerous
and disciplined enough
to never misuse that danger.

A King does not ask to be followed.
He becomes undeniable.

I am Seven.
I have spoken.
Now ask yourself—
by whose voice do you rise?

The Board

A kingdom is not land.
It is discipline, order, and responsibility.

A throne is not sat on.
It is earned — and defended daily.

Chess teaches men what life hides:

Not everyone is a king.
Not everyone wants to be.
And most who say they do are lying to themselves.

A king stands alone more often than he stands adored.
Leadership is not applause — it is pressure.

Pawns
Humble men who move forward with courage.
The world mocks them —
but kingdoms fall without them.

Knights
Brothers.
Unpredictable. Loyal.
They ride toward danger without flinching.
A king does not survive without men who will bleed at his flank.

Bishops
Advisors with insight and ambition.
Wisdom has shadows.
A king listens —
but trusts only action, not counsel.

Rooks
Silent strength.
Sentinels.
They anchor the realm.
They do not speak much —
they do their duty.

The Queen
Not ruled — aligned.
Her power is not granted by him —
it is **recognized by him**.
Grace, fire, intuition, loyalty.
A wise king protects her.
A wise queen protects the mission.

Enemies come.
Allies fade.
Weak men fold.
Purpose stands.

A king does not seek peace —
he maintains it by readiness for war.

A queen does not seek attention —
she expands the kingdom in silence.

A king who serves his mission becomes unshakeable.
A queen who serves with him becomes unforgettable.

The board is always in motion.
Your life is the strategy.
Your discipline is the defense.
Your legacy is the checkmate.

Move with intention.
Command without shouting.
Stand without boasting.
Lead without begging.

Let others chase status.
You chase truth.

The world bows
not to the loudest man,
but to the one who cannot be moved.

The Queen

A Queen is not chosen.
She reveals herself.

Not through noise,
not through demands,
but through **presence, discernment, and restraint**.

A Queen does not chase attention —
she commands respect by existing in **quiet power**.

Her softness is not weakness;
it is strategy.
Her tenderness is not submission;
it is **control over chaos**.

A girl competes with the world.
A Queen **conquers herself** first.

She is not led by impulse, envy, or pride.
She builds, she nurtures, she sharpens—
and she expects the same in return.

A Queen is not defined by men,
but she knows the power of alignment with a worthy one.

She does not kneel —
she chooses where she stands.

Her loyalty is not given —
it is earned and guarded like a crown.

Her submission, when given,
is not obedience—
it is **devotion to a mission greater than ego**.

She does not crave a throne for vanity.
She carries one in her soul.
A true King does not need to place a crown on her head—
he simply acknowledges the one she already wears.

She does not stir war in his peace,
and he does not dim her fire.

She matches his steadiness,
his discipline,
his forward motion.

Together, they become dual force:

Steel and silk.
Fire and water.
Earth and sky.
Power and grace in balance.

She is not his shadow —
she is his equal horizon.

And when they stand together,
the world does not ask who leads.
It simply steps aside.

The King's Burden

A King is not crowned by comfort.
He is carved by responsibility.

Leadership is not about glory.
It is the weight no one else wants to carry
and the silence no one else can endure.

A king doesn't stand above others —
he stands **in front** of them
when storms arrive.

He sacrifices first.
He hurts privately.
He bleeds quietly.
He remains steady when every voice around him cracks.

The world believes kings enjoy power.
They do not see the cost:

The decisions no one wants to make.
The battles no one else can fight.
The enemies that are not people,
but doubts, temptations, and ghosts from wars internal and external.

A king does not wake up wanting command.
He wakes up **unable to abandon it.**

Kings are not chosen by desire.
They are chosen by endurance.
Not by perfection —
but by the courage to face imperfection head-on
and lead anyway.

A king carries legacy on his spine.
A man collapses from ego;
a king survives through discipline.

A king is not feared by the world
because he shouts.
He is feared because he **cannot be moved**.

Strength is not anger.
Strength is stillness.
Strength is choosing mission
over mood, moment, and impulse.

A king knows this truth:

Power without duty is corruption.
Power with duty is destiny.

And so he walks —
not because he is unafraid,
but because he refuses to bow
to anything less
than who he must become.

He Changed

I was a good man once.
Simple.
Straight-lined.
Heart clean.
Eyes open.
Dreams bigger than reality had any right to allow.

Then war taught me something the world never warned me about:

**Violence doesn't change you
as much as it reveals you.**

They trained me to survive hell,
then expected me to smile in peace
like nothing ever happened.

You come home and everyone pretends
life snaps back into place.
It doesn't.
You don't.

War rewires a man.
Not because he wants it to—
because innocence is a casualty long before the body count starts.

People say,
"He changed."

No.
I adapted.
You would too, if you saw how fast heaven turns into blood and noise.

I wasn't angry at the world.
I was cautious of it
because I knew exactly what I was capable of

if someone pushed too far.

That doesn't make you dangerous.
That makes you honest.

The truth is simple:

I was a good man.
Then duty shaped me into a necessary version of myself.

Good men don't stay good in war.
They stay alive.
They protect who they can.
They bury who they couldn't.
Then they come home carrying ghosts
no one else can see.

Not broken.
Not lost.
Different.

And difference scares people—
because they don't know what it cost you to become it.

Boots

Sometimes when I sit alone,
I hear them again —
the boots.

Not one pair.
Not a squad.
A tide.
A generation in cadence.

Young men with fresh bones
and unscarred minds,
believing discipline could make them immortal
and courage could make them right.

The clatter of those boots was a promise:
We were willing.
We were ready.
We belonged to something bigger than ourselves.

There was sunlight in those days,
even when war was waiting in the wings.
Laughing in formation,
complaining about nothing and everything,
pretending we weren't afraid —
and becoming men before we ever got the chance to be boys.

Only those who've heard that march
feel it still in their chest —
a drum you never truly put down.

Training wasn't about killing.
It was about preparing to die
without breaking in front of each other.

People think the battlefield makes the soldier.
They're wrong.
Boots marching in peace
toward a future painted in uncertainty —
that's where the warrior is born.

Some of those boots never came home.
Some came home in silence.
Some returned in pieces, breathing but altered.

We learned early that time is a luxury
and brotherhood is a debt.

Those boots belonged to boys who walked forward
knowing the world would never thank them
and walked anyway.

Today, I sit in quiet rooms
and hear echoes of cadence,
not because I mourn the past —
but because I honor the ones
who gave their youth to a country
that never looked them in the eye long enough
to understand the cost.

They weren't fearless.
They marched anyway.

And that is courage.

Controlled Chaos

Violence lives in every man.
But only a few ever meet their own capacity for it.

A criminal stumbles into violence.
A soldier is trained to walk into it with purpose.

One reacts.
The other **decides**.

People think the difference is morality.
They're wrong.
The difference is **discipline.**

A soldier learns to control destruction,
to direct force,
to carry violence like a loaded weapon
he prays he never has to draw—
but will, without hesitation, if the mission demands.

A criminal chases chaos.
A soldier manages it.
One is driven by ego;
the other by duty.

But here's the truth nobody likes:

The line between them is thin.
Thinner than society admits.
Thinner than the world wants to see.

War doesn't make good men bad.
It introduces them to the darkness inside them—
the same darkness that lives in everyone—
and demands they master it instead of pretending it isn't there.

That's the part civilians never understand.
They think violence is measured in action.
In shots fired.
In blood spilled.

Real violence is measured in restraint.
In the chaos you *didn't* unleash.
In the trigger you held steady.
In the anger you learned to swallow
because you knew what would happen if you didn't.

A criminal breaks because he never learned control.
A soldier breaks because he learned it too well.

We are not defined by the battles we fought—
but by the ones we refused to start.

Discipline is the difference.
Duty is the anchor.
And the quiet truth is this:

Anyone can be dangerous.
Only the honorable learn when **not** to be.

Returning Fire

I didn't realize when it happened —
the moment the man I was stopped living
and the man I became took his place.

They say war changes you.
That's easy to say when you've never felt it happen —
slow, quiet, permanent —
like gravity shifting inside your skull.

One day, you look in the mirror
and realize you don't know the eyes looking back.
Not fully.
Not anymore.

There's sadness in that.
Not self-pity —
just truth.

I didn't die out there.
But parts of me never made it home.
Parts I miss more than people will ever understand.

People think violence breaks men.
They're wrong.

What breaks a man
is learning he can return fire with no hesitation—
and knowing that instinct doesn't turn off
just because the war ended.

Everyone talks about danger
like it's a thing outside themselves.
They don't know how it feels
to fear what you might do
if someone pushes a little too hard,
talks a little too loud,
touches the wrong nerve.

That's the heartbreak.
Not the violence—
the awareness.

You come back trying to fit into a world
built out of comfort and noise,
where people mistake softness for virtue
and have never tasted their own edge.

You laugh in the right places,
say the right things,
go through the motions of "normal."
And inside there's a quiet, steady hum:

"Stay calm.
Stay in control.
They don't know what you know."

I'm not ashamed of who I became.
I'm not broken.
I adapted.
I survived.
I carry things others will never have to carry.

But sometimes, late in the evening,
when memory walks in uninvited,
I grieve the man who didn't know
how heavy life could get.

I don't want him back.
He wouldn't survive this world.
He's gone.

And that hurts.

But I stand anyway.

Steel doesn't mourn the ore it used to be.
It just remembers the fire
that forged it.

Capacity

People think strength is loud.
That danger announces itself.

It doesn't.
Real danger is quiet, measured, breathing slow.
It sits in the room politely,
because it doesn't need to posture.

I don't fear anyone.
I fear **reverting**.

I know exactly how fast a situation can turn,
how quickly instinct can outrun thought,
how violence doesn't ask for permission—
it arrives, it moves, and it remembers.

That's why I stay calm.
Not because I'm weak,
but because I have already met the version of myself
that doesn't stop once he starts.

People think I avoid conflict because I'm intimidated.
Truth is, I avoid conflict because I respect what I'm capable of.

There is no pride in destruction.
There is only aftermath.
Paperwork.
Regret.
A hollow room and a long night replaying decisions.

So I choose peace.
Not because I'm soft,
but because I've seen what the other choice costs.

I don't raise my voice.
I don't puff my chest.
I don't threaten.

I watch.
I measure.
I breathe.

A seasoned wolf doesn't snarl.
He simply knows what will happen if he must bite.

That's discipline.
That's restraint.
That's survival.

And if you see me walk away,
you aren't watching surrender.
You're watching **mercy**.

Not for you—
for the man I promised myself I would never become again
unless there was no other choice.

A peaceful man isn't harmless.
He is a man who made peace
with the fact that harm is always an option—
and chose mastery instead.

Good Man

I was a good man
Til it all went bad
I was a good man
This life is so sad

The pressures of being honest and true
Become too much to bare when it's only you
Against the world and everyone on the same side
They come against you glaring with their eyes opened wide

They see right thru you knowing you don't belong
Inevitably they all know the lyrics of the same song
You don't fit in know matter how hard you try
This isn't the life you were meant to live it's only a lie

You wanted to fit in and tried to get in
But you were never in and at the end
You were only left regrettin
The choices you made while you were pretendin
To being something you weren't when
All you became was locked in
A way life that had you whisperin
Dear lord when will it all end

I was a good man
Til it all went bad
I was a good man
This life is so sad

The Moth

I was called to you by the brightness you imposed on the world
I was drawn in by the perceived pleasures and passions
You enticed me with the glow of your warmth and energy
I came to the realization too late of your true nature and effects
Now I lay here trapped with no means for escape
I'm now doomed to perish in your burning flames by my own desires

Rest In Peace for Today I Die

I wanted to tell her and show her how much I loved her
Seemingly she was always unable or unwilling to accept my hear for fear
The pain is deep and a festering, in-healing wound of betrayal that
The pain is real, man I just wanted peace

Why do I obsess over you when you clearly cast me aside without regard
I just want to die inside because this shit is way too hard
I wonder if you'll ever know the depth of my love for you
So sad knowing how sick you are in your own twisted head

In the end I know it isn't your fault for the way that your mind works and the perception of reality
Life is cruel and nature is her strong executioner
Growing up listening to all those love songs, Marvin Gaye, Keith sweat, jodeci

Got me all fucked up. I'd rather be on some Hennessy
I'm dead inside, this is my final cry

I've thought about my last night on earth Rest In Peace for today I die

Cold Burn

I know you hate me; I hate me
Fuck this world; it's a cold burn

Time moves on; we grow older and there's never enough in the lessons we learn.

I'm no-one, nothing at all in the thoughts that pursue me.
Damn I just wanted you and I did all I could do and still you left me.
Why you hate me I'll never know
Is it the love inside me
That makes you run from me

I'm so lost; I'm such a liar
It's burned deep and burned itself out;
there's no more fire.
The flame is gone and all is lost; you were my only desire.

With you I always felt so free.
In my mind we were a perfect unity.
I thought we'd be together throughout eternity.
Now the heavens have come together to judge us evenly.

You hate; I hate.
Fuck you. Die violently you piece of shit.
All the anger inside of me you inspire in a constant state of play.
The games we played have brought us to our final fate.

This is our fate
You're sick in the head; twisted addict
Fucked yourself and left crying through the day
All that we have left of one another is the hate.

I know you hate me; I hate me
Fuck this world; it's a cold burn

It all came crashing down.
We destroyed the only love we could've ever known.
Now we're left to drown
In our own agony you're gone

It's a slow burn
That takes its toll as the world turn
I'm finally done and careworn
Just take my ashes and find my final resting place in a golden urn

I know you hate me; I hate me
Fuck this world; it's a cold burn

Time moves on; we grow older and there's never enough in the lessons we learn.

I'm no-one, nothing at all in the thoughts that pursue me.
Damn I just wanted you and I did all I could do and still you left me.
Why you hate me I'll never know
Is it the love inside me
That makes run from me

I'm so lost; I'm such a liar
It's burned deep and burned itself out;
there's no more fire.
The flame is gone and all is lost; you were my only desire.

With you I always felt so free.
In my mind we were a perfect unity.
I thought we'd be together throughout eternity.
Now the heavens have come together to judge us evenly.

You hate; I hate.
Fuck you. Die violently you piece of shit.
All the anger inside of me you inspire in a constant state of play.
The games we played have brought us to our final fate.

This is our fate
You're sick in the head; twisted addict
Fucked yourself and left crying through the day
All that we have left of one another is the hate.

I know you hate me; I hate me
Fuck this world; it's a cold burn

It all came crashing down.
We destroyed the only love we could've ever known.
Now we're left to drown
In our own agony you're gone

It's a slow burn
That takes its toll as the world turn
I'm finally done and careworn
Just take my ashes and find my final resting place in a golden urn

She Hung There

They found her hanging.
Not peaceful,
not floating toward light or angels or comfort—
just still,
finally done running from the pain that chased her
from birth.

Some people are not destroyed by choices.
They are destroyed by **conditions**.
Born into storms, raised in absence,
fed by neglect instead of love.

People love to judge the broken.
They forget some children never see safety,
never know softness,
never learn how to breathe without fear.

She was one of those souls.

A father gone before memory formed.
A mother present only in biology,
never in warmth.
Home after home,
none of them ever "home."

You can only grow so strong
when you were never watered.

She chased love like oxygen,
and men mistook that hunger for weakness.
They blamed her for drowning
when she had never been taught to swim.

Every heartbreak,
every abandonment,
every lie she held against her ribs
became another stone in her pockets.

And yes—
she made mistakes.
Hurt others.
Chose badly.
Fell apart in public.
Not because she was cruel—
but because life never taught her how to hold herself together.

When she finally tied the rope,
the world didn't stop.
It rarely does for the wounded.

There is no poetry in her ending.
No romance in tragedy.
Just a girl who never felt safe,
finally choosing silence over screaming.

And still—
I don't judge her.
I mourn her.
Not the act,
but the life she never had the chance to grow into.

Some people break
because nobody ever showed them
how to bend without shattering.

And if there is a God watching,
I hope He greeted her gently—
the way this world never did.

Loving the Broken

Some people are born behind the curve of grace.
Life hits them first,
and often, hardest.

And when you love someone like that —
someone carved by pain instead of comfort,
shaped by survival instead of safety —
you learn a brutal truth:

**Not everyone you love
has the tools to love you back.**

It's not malice.
Or betrayal.
Or a choice to harm.

Sometimes it's simply this:
they never learned how to hold their own hurt,
so they hand it to whoever stands closest.

Pain makes people dangerous.
Not because they want to be —
but because drowning people
don't know they're pulling you under
while they fight for air.

Loving the broken isn't romantic.
It is devotion etched in sorrow,
watching someone battle demons
they don't recognize aren't you.

And the worst part isn't losing them.
The worst part is knowing
there was a version of them that never got to exist —
one you glimpsed
in small, rare, beautiful moments
between storms.

The world will tell you to harden.
To hate them.
To move on and forget.

But the truth is simpler and heavier:

Some souls never got a fair start.
And loving them will break pieces of you,
you didn't know could crack.

But that doesn't make you weak.
It makes you human.

I don't regret loving the wounded.
I regret a world that creates them
and then mocks them for bleeding.

And when the darkness comes,
and memory aches,
I remind myself:

**You can walk through hell
without becoming fire.**

Some of us learned compassion
the hard way —
by holding those the world abandoned
and still choosing light
after they let go.

Look Away

We live in a world where people bleed in public
and the crowd watches like it's entertainment.

Suffering isn't sacred anymore.
It's content.
A clip to swipe past.
A caption to skim.
A punchline for people who have forgotten
they are just as human as the ones they mock.

When someone cracks,
cries for help,
breaks under the weight of a world they never asked to carry—
most don't offer a hand.
They offer judgment.
Or worse, indifference.

It shouldn't surprise me.
Comfort breeds numbness.
Screens build distance.
People look away because feeling costs energy
and empathy feels like an inconvenience now.

Still… it stings.
Not for me.
For us.
For what we are becoming.

Once, pain meant community.
Now it means isolation
and public silence
behind private storms.

I've seen men die in dirt
and others die in living rooms
with no one noticing the difference.

I've watched proud souls collapse quietly
because asking for help felt like losing.
And no one thought to ask if they were okay.

People say,
"If you need anything, I'm here,"
but they never mean it.
They mean
as long as it's easy, brief, and requires nothing real from me.

I don't hate them for it.
I don't curse them.
I just see them—
fragile humans trained by comfort
to fear discomfort.

And I choose differently.
Because a man isn't measured
by how he stands when he is strong,
but by whether he kneels beside the broken
when no one else does.

If the world looks away,
be the one who turns toward.

Not to save everyone—
that's God's work, not ours—
but to stay human
in a time when numbness passes for strength.

There is still honor in caring,
even when the world forgets how.

After the Fall

There are moments in a man's life
when he looks around and realizes
he no longer recognizes the ground he's standing on —
or the man standing on it.

Not because the world changed,
but because **he did**.

Pain doesn't announce itself.
It erodes.
Quiet, patient, patient as winter
until one day you wake up and understand
you are not who you were
and cannot go back to who you will never be again.

People think losing yourself looks dramatic.
It doesn't.
It looks like routine.
Like daily function.
Like showing up on time
while a version of you bleeds quietly
under your ribs.

One day, you break.
Not loud —
clean.
Internal.
A fracture no one sees but you.

And then comes the hardest part:
not surviving the loss,
but **living after it**.

There is a season
where you walk through the ruins of your old self
like a soldier clearing a battlefield —
methodical, quiet, eyes open
not for enemies,
but for whatever pieces are still worth keeping.

No anger.
No dramatic collapse.
Just **truth**.

I was someone once.
I am someone else now.
And the bridge between those men
was fire.

Do I miss him?
Sometimes.
But nostalgia is a gentle liar.
He would not have survived what I know now.

So I don't mourn him.
I honor him.
He fell so I could stand.

Losing yourself isn't the tragedy.
Refusing to build again is.

A man does not stay rubble.
A man sifts the ashes,
keeps what still holds weight,
and rebuilds —
not into who he was,
but into who the pain required him to become.

That's not weakness.
That's **continuation.**

Not reborn.
Not redeemed.
Just **still here** —
and that is enough.

Unashamed

There comes a point when a man stops arguing with his past
and starts accepting his reflection —
not as victory, not as failure,
just as **truth**.

I am who I am.
Not who people expected.
Not who I once pretended to be.
Not the ideal version I held in my head
before life taught me humility and consequence.

I've been the hero in my own story,
and the villain in someone else's.
I've hurt and been hurt.
Loved recklessly, fought blindly,
stood tall, fallen hard,
and crawled when pride said I should walk.

And yet I stand.

There is a certain peace
in no longer needing to be understood.
In knowing your flaws
and sharpening them into awareness instead of shame.

A man who lies to himself
is already lost.
A man who knows himself
cannot be owned.

Vulnerability isn't weakness —
it's honesty without theatrics.
It's saying:
I've been broken,
but I didn't stay broken.
I've been wrong,
but I learned.
I bleed,
but I heal.

That's not narcissism.
That's survival without self-deception.

I am not perfect.
I don't need to be.
Perfection is a costume,
and I outgrew pretending.

Some will call it hardness.
Others will call it ego.
Let them.

Strength rarely gets labeled correctly
by people who've never had to build it.

I am not ashamed of who I became
to survive what I lived.

You don't earn peace by hiding your scars.
You earn it by owning your name,
your choices,
your shadow,
and your light —
and walking forward anyway.

Unapologetic.
Not proud, not regretful —
just **true**.

I am me.
And that is enough.

What Hurt Made

People love to say pain makes you stronger.
That's only half the truth.
Pain offers the opportunity —
strength is whether you rise or rot.

I didn't get better because life hurt me.
I got better because I refused to stay broken.
There's a difference.

There was a time I didn't recognize myself —
not because I changed for the worse,
but because I didn't yet understand who I had to become.

Losing yourself isn't the tragedy.
Staying lost is.

Pain stripped me.
It took pieces I thought were permanent.
Dreams.
Naivety.
Softness I didn't know I had until it was gone.

And for a while, I mourned that man.
Not because he was better —
but because he was simpler,
untouched by the weight that would eventually shape him.

Grief for the old self is real.
So is gratitude for the new one.

I don't worship my wounds.
I don't pretend scars are holy.
Pain didn't save me —
discipline did.
Reflection did.
Refusal to die emotionally when life tried to bury me did.

I don't wear suffering like a medal.
I carry it like a tool —
kept sharp, used when needed,
never the whole of who I am.

Pain didn't make me noble.
Work did.
Humility did.
The courage to rebuild did.

I am not who I was.
I am not who I could've been if life was gentle.

I am what remained.
And what I decided to build
from what remained.

Not defined by the fire —
defined by walking through it
and not letting it name me.

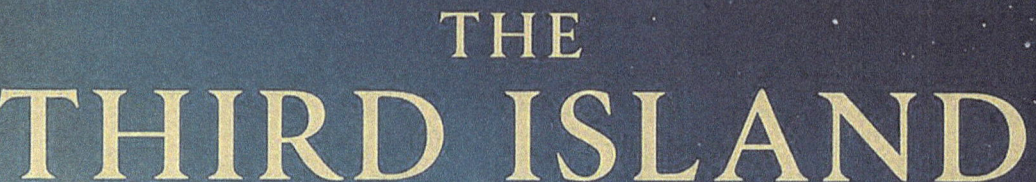

THE THIRD ISLAND

THE ISLAND OF EARTH

THE ISLAND OF MEN

THE ISLAND OF THE MIND AND SPIRIT

The Third Island

There are three worlds a man must learn to walk through.

The Island of Earth

The physical world.
Where bodies matter, bills exist, hunger is real,
and nature answers only to truth.

Here, strength is built through sweat,
discipline through repetition,
humility through time.

A man learns he is mortal here —
and learns to earn what he eats.

The Island of Men

The systems we build.
Countries, laws, culture, ego, status, noise.
This is where people fight over illusions
and call it purpose.

Here you learn politics,
power games,
selfishness disguised as virtue,
and virtue mocked like weakness.

This world crowns cowards
and ignores saints.
Learn to move through it
without letting it rewrite you.

Most men get trapped in one of these two.
Chasing survival or validation
with no space left for soul.

But there is a third place,
quiet and infinite:

The Island of the Mind and Spirit

You do not travel to it —
you remember it.

This is where a man meets himself
without distraction or applause.
Where silence stops feeling empty
and starts feeling honest.

This island is where you face your ghosts,
where pride dies,
where peace begins.

Here you understand:

The body is temporary.
Society is theater.
But the mind —
the soul —
that is kingdom.

Here you learn the first law of power:

If you cannot command yourself,
you cannot command anything.

Here, God is not distant —
He is encountered
in breath, in discipline, in stillness,
in the stubborn refusal to become bitter
no matter how often the world gives you reason.

A man who lives only in the body
becomes an animal.
A man who lives only in society
becomes a puppet.
A man who learns the third island
becomes **sovereign.**

Travel between all three.
Honor each realm.
But build your throne
in the one no one can invade.

That is where freedom lives.
And freedom is the only crown worth wearing.

Like No One Else

I treat my fellow man like shit,
Why for?
Because it makes me feel legit,
I often ponder and wonder,
Why can't I quit?

Alas the reason,
I'll have a look at myself,
taking heed to every season,
I'm at war within,
committing acts of treason.

I'll never truly live,
While blaming others,
Constantly, unwilling to forgive,
Only when until I let go,
And freely give.

This is what I've come to determine,
Accepting myself for who I am.
Understanding that I'm only human,
To forgive myself of all things,
And love myself like none one else can,

The Discipline of Peace

Real warriors do not brag about strength.
They do not chase conflict.
They do not raise their voice to prove a point
or swing fists to protect their pride.

They know what they are capable of.
They've seen what rage can do.
They've held violence in their hands
and learned it listens to no one once released.

So they choose peace.
Not out of fear—
but out of **respect**
for what sleeps inside them.

The loudest men are often the weakest,
mistaking noise for power,
mistaking chaos for courage.

A true warrior has nothing to prove.
He does not posture.
He does not beg for validation.
He does not need recognition.

He knows the difference
between walking away because he is afraid to fight,
and walking away because he refuses
to waste himself on battles beneath him.

Peace is not passivity.
Peace is **control**.
Peace is **strength on a leash**.
Peace is the power to say:

"I could... but I won't."

Not out of mercy for others,
but out of loyalty to himself.

Anger is easy.
Retaliation is instinct.
Violence is simple once you've tasted it.

But restraint—
that is the mark of a man who commands himself.

I don't aim to be feared.
I aim to be **unmoved**.
Steady in storms.
Calm in conflict.
Centered when others shake.

Because peace isn't the absence of battle.
It's the discipline to only fight
when the cause is worthy
and the mission demands it.

And the ones I speak to now—
men learning to carry their strength—
listen carefully:

Do not chase war
when you haven't yet mastered yourself.
The battlefield begins within.

Win there first.
Then the world cannot break you.

Peace is not weakness.
It is the final form of strength.

Build Yourself

No one becomes who they want to be by accident.
You do not drift into strength.
You do not stumble into purpose.
You do not wake up one day forged—
you burn for it.

Decide who you are.
Not who you *wish* to be.
Who you **must become**
to earn peace, power, and self-respect.

Identity is not found.
It is **built**.
Brick by brutal brick,
truth stacked on truth,
habit welded to discipline,
morning by morning,
rep by rep,
moment by moment.

Weak men wait for motivation.
Strong men move without it.

The world doesn't crown the emotional.
It crowns the consistent.

This life will break you if you let it.
So don't let it.
Stand up before you feel ready.
Move before you feel strong.
Act before you feel motivated.

No one cares how tired you are.
No one cares how heavy your past feels.
And life will not slow down
because you are wounded.

It is your duty
to rise anyway.

Look in the mirror and tell yourself the truth:
I am not done.
I am not finished.
I am not defeated.

Then build the man who can back those words.

Suffer on purpose.
Choose the hard path.
Lift what tries to crush you.
Run until your excuses break.
Sit in silence until your demons choke on it.
Forgive when you could hate.
Stand when you want to fold.
Speak only what you live.

The world will doubt you.
Good.
Let their disbelief be fuel.

You have one life.
One mind.
One chance to be formidable.

Stop waiting to feel ready.
Earn readiness through action.
Pick up your purpose like a weapon
and march.

Every day you choose discipline,
you choose destiny.

Be who you said you'd be.
And when you fail,
stand again.

That's the work.
That's the way.
That's the only path worth walking.

Build yourself.
Or be built by circumstance.
One is honor.
The other is surrender.

And you are not here to surrender.

The Higher Ground

I used to think strength was force.
Winning.
Dominating.
Standing taller than whoever stood across from me.

That was before I learned power without direction is just noise,
and pride without purpose is just insecurity wearing armor.

True strength isn't in who you can break.
It's in who you can **protect**,
who you can **forgive**,
and what you can walk away from
without losing yourself.

There is a kind of love that has nothing to do with softness.
It's discipline.
It's control.
It's saying:

I see what you tried to do.
I feel what it could make me become.
And I will choose something higher
because I refuse to become lesser.

It's easy to hate.
Easy to rage.
Easy to point at the world and call it broken
while becoming just another sharp edge in the debris.

But a man who has seen violence,
who has stood inside chaos,
who has tasted the kind of power that can end a life or reshape one —
he knows:

the dangerous man who chooses restraint
is the safest man to walk with.

I don't hold the higher ground because I think I'm better.
I hold it because I know myself.
Because I know what I could be
if I let bitterness make my choices for me.

It's not weakness to seek peace.
It's wisdom.

Anyone can throw a fist.
Few can hold one
and not use it
just because pride is hungry.

Courage is not only charging forward.
Sometimes courage is staying still.
Seeing the insult, the disrespect, the ignorance —
and refusing to offer your spirit to pettiness.

I don't love people because they're good.
I love them because **I choose to remain human**
in a world that forgets what that means.

The higher ground is not a mountain you stand on.
It's a fight inside you —
every day, every look, every decision.

Take it not for applause,
but because dignity is something you build alone in the quiet.
And when the world claws at you,
you do not claw back.

You stand.
You breathe.
And you stay bigger than what tried to shrink you.

That is honor.
That is strength.
That is the only victory worth having.

The Warrior Who Knows Himself

Steel does not boast.
It simply holds its edge.

Fire does not apologize for burning.
It simply learns where to rest.

The ocean does not announce its depth.
It swallows mountains in silence.

I do not need to roar.
I have roared.
I know the price.

Strength untested is posture.
Strength survived is quiet.

Power speaks softly
because it remembers the cost of raising its voice.

Violence is not the enemy.
Lack of control is.

Peace is not softness.
Peace is mastery.

I do not avoid the storm.
I **am** the storm
disciplined into direction.

My anger is trained,
my heart is scarred,
my hands know both
destruction and mercy.

I could break.
I have broken.
Yet here I stand
unbroken.

A king does not chase war.
A warrior does not chase harm.
The strong do not chase approval.
The awakened do not chase ego.

I carry the sword
but draw it only for purpose.

I carry wounds
but bleed only in truth.

I carry power
but worship restraint.

Everything that tried to destroy me
made the ground beneath me stronger.

I am not here to prove I can fight.
I am here to **prove I don't have to.**

The world does not control me.
My shadow does not own me.
My past does not define me.

I am dangerous.
I am disciplined.
I am whole.

I am the warrior
who knows himself.

Character Is the Spine

A man's worth is not in what he lifts,
but what he refuses to drop.

Power means nothing
if you bend for every temptation
and break for every fear.

Character is not armor.
It is **spine**.

When storms come,
it does not pray to be spared —
it stands and lets the wind learn its name.

I do not chase respect.
I live in a way
that makes it inevitable.

I hold myself
to the version of me
I promised I would become.

Strength without virtue is failure.
Strength with humility is legacy.

On Loving Through the Flaws

There is beauty in imperfection
and danger in denial.

To see someone's wounds
and not weaponize them—
that is loyalty.

To look at someone's darkness
and still choose light—
that is love.

Not blind,
not naive—
aware,
and still willing.

The world breaks the gentle first,
but it forgets the gentle
are the ones who rebuild it.

Be firm.
Be kind.
Be unshaken
and unpoisoned.

It costs nothing to be cruel.
It costs everything
to remain human
after life has taught you to bite.

Higher Ground is a Choice

Most people don't take the high road.
Not because they don't know where it is,
but because they'd rather feel clever than be honorable.

Retaliation feels good in the moment.
Character feels good forever.

I don't stay calm because I'm soft.
I stay calm because losing my center
is a luxury I don't allow myself.

Anyone can throw a punch.
Anyone can spit venom.
Anyone can escalate.

But to stand still in the fire,
to breathe while others burn,
to choose silence over ego
and compassion over pride—

that is war most men will never win.

If you want to conquer the world,
first conquer your reactions.

That is where kings are crowned.

The Ground Rules

- Earn respect — never demand it.
- Speak truth — especially when it costs you.
- Control your emotions — or they control you.
- Love deeply — but never without boundaries.
- Forgive — not to release them, but to free you.
- Move with intention — not impulse.
- Stand alone if you must — but never bend for lies.
- Leave every room stronger than you found it.
- Lead yourself first — or don't call it leadership.
- If you break, rebuild quietly — and come back harder.

Honor is not something you talk about.
It's something you carry.

A Man Dies When His Purpose Does

Legacy Is a Burden Men Carry Quietly

Legacy isn't loud.
It doesn't beg to be seen.
It isn't a speech,
or a statue,
or applause.

Legacy is built in silence:
in choices no one praises,
in sacrifices no one sees,
in discipline when nobody's watching.

A man dies twice:
once when his body falls,
and again when his name loses meaning.

Fight for something
that outlives your pulse.

Inheritance Is Character First, Results Second

Most men think legacy is accomplishment.
Money.
Trophies.
Recognition.
Followers.
A highlight reel they imagine the world will remember.

But real legacy doesn't start outside your life.
It starts inside your habits.

Legacy is integrity that outlasts trends.
Discipline that survives fatigue.
Values that hold when temptation hits.
A spine that doesn't bend to noise.

Legacy is the echo of who you trained yourself to become.

You don't leave legacy by talking.
You leave it by living a life worth studying.

You owe the future version of you —
and the ones who walk after you —
a man who didn't collapse into comfort
when life demanded courage.

Kingship is not ruling.
It is **responsibility in motion**.
It is understanding that someone, someday,
will live in the world you helped shape,
even if your name never passes their lips.

Legacy is not credit.
It is contribution.

Not fame.
Footprints.

Not immortality.
Impact.

Quiet Builders

Not every great man is remembered.
Not every loud man is great.

Some men become legend.
Some men become foundation.
Both matter.

The world is held up
by names never spoken,
sacrifices never recorded,
quiet courage never applauded.

Every generation survives because
some men built instead of bragged,
stood instead of posed,
worked instead of whined,
held the line
when quitting was fashionable.

Greatness doesn't always get a headline.
But it always leaves a footprint.

The Duty of a Man Who Thinks Beyond Himself

- Live as if a child you love is watching every choice.
- Build habits worthy of inheritance.
- Protect what is sacred — family, truth, dignity.
- Refuse shortcuts — legacy can't be hacked.
- Speak only what your actions can defend.
- Sacrifice is the tax for meaning.
- Make peace with being misunderstood; legacy is seldom recognized in real-time.
- Strength is not for status — it's for service.
- What you build in yourself becomes your offering to time.
- Do not fear being forgotten — fear being forgettable.

Legacy is not about being seen.
It's about **leaving something that would not exist without you**.

And carrying that weight
without needing applause.

The God of Men Who've Seen Violence

I do not fear God.
I **respect** Him.

Fear is for men who run from themselves.
I have faced myself in the mirror,
and I know what darkness is capable of.

If God wanted blind obedience,
He would have made soldiers,
not men.

Instead, He gave us choice,

conscience,

fire,

and consequence.

This world is not gentle.
Neither is its Creator.
But there is a difference between cruelty and forging.

Steel does not become steel
without heat.

I used to think strength meant bearing every burden alone.
Now I know pride can be a prison disguised as armor.

God is not found in begging.
God is not found in shouting scripture.
God is not found in fear of punishment.

God is found
when the battle is over,
when the room goes quiet,
and the echoes of who you could have become
sit across from who you decided to be.

And you sit with it.
And you do not run.

That is when you hear Him.

Not in thunder.
In breath.
In discipline.
In the quiet refusal to surrender to bitterness.

I do not ask God to carry my weight.
I ask for the strength to carry it myself
and the wisdom to know what to lay down.

Forgiveness is not forgetting.
It is releasing the impulse to destroy
what harmed you.

Mercy is not softness.
It is command of self.

A man who cannot forgive
is still owned by his enemy.

A man who refuses the higher path
is still ruled by his pain.

I do not worship blindly.
I walk with God like a soldier walks with a commander
he has bled beside:

Not always agreeing,
not always understanding,
but trusting the mission is bigger than me.

I have seen death.
I have heard screaming.
I have felt hate burn hotter than gunfire.

And still—

I choose peace.

Not because I am weak,
but because strength without grace
is just another form of war.

My faith is simple:

God is real.
The world is brutal.
And I am responsible for who I become between the two.

I do not kneel out of fear.
I kneel out of discipline.

Because any man who has carried a weapon
knows the holiest act
is learning when not to draw it.

Redemption Is a Discipline

Redemption is not granted.
Redemption is earned.

Not through apologies,
but through consistency.

Not through regret,
but through responsibility.

A man is not redeemed by tears —
only by **change**.

You do not escape who you were
by wishing for who you want to be.

You rise
by clawing yourself out,
inch by inch,
day by day,
choice by choice.

Fall if you must.
Fail if you will.
But **rise with your eyes open.**

Accountability Is a Form of Prayer

Everyone loves the idea of second chances —
until they're asked to earn one.

People talk about forgiveness
like it's a switch you flip,
like redemption is automatic
if you feel bad enough.

No.

Redemption is a discipline.

You don't get a new life
because you regret the old one.

You build a new life
by killing the parts of you
that kept you small, angry, impulsive, weak.

That's the real repentance —
not suffering in shame,
but standing up and living differently.

Accountability is a form of prayer.
Not to some distant God,
but to the man you promised to become.

You want forgiveness?
Earn it with action.
Earn it by showing up.
Earn it by refusing to go backwards
even when backwards feels familiar.

You don't rise by hating who you were.
You rise by refusing to stay him.

The Climb Back

Redemption is not light breaking through clouds.
It is you lighting a candle in your own darkness
and carrying it —
even when your hands shake.

It is the silence after regret,
where you choose who speaks —
the shame
or the future.

It is patience with yourself,
and violence toward your excuses.

It is looking at the pieces you broke
and building something stronger
from the shards.

Real redemption is slow.
Ugly.
Steady.
Earned quietly.

By the time people notice,
you'll already be standing.

Rules for Rising

- Do not justify your failures — correct them.
- Do not drown in guilt — transform it into discipline.
- Do not beg for trust — build it brick by brick.
- One honest step forward is worth more than a thousand regrets.
- Never waste pain — repurpose it.
- Own what you did.
- Forgive yourself only after you outgrow who did it.
- Judge yourself by your actions, not your intentions.
- Redemption favors the stubborn.
- The world forgives the man who refuses to stop rising.

Redemption is not a second chance.
It is becoming someone who didn't waste the first.

www.ingramcontent.com/pod-product-compliance
Lightning Source LLC
Chambersburg PA
CBHW081452180426
43194CB00054B/2807